MACAO PARALLEL WORLDS

澳門 平行世界

Edited by Wang Shu & Lu Wenyu
編著: 王澍 & 陸文宇

Photographs by Iwan Baan
攝影: 伊萬 · 巴恩

CULTURAL AFFAIRS BUREAU
OF THE MACAO SAR GOVERNMENT
LARS MÜLLER PUBLISHERS

Old Town 老城
Casino City 賭城
New City 新城

MESSAGE

O Lam

Secretary for Social Affairs and Culture of the
Macao Special Administrative Region Government

The Venice International Architecture Biennale is a world-renowned event celebrating architectural, artistic and cultural exchange. Since its debut in 2014, Macao, China has showcased its unique cultural charm and architectural wisdom at the Biennale, contributing new voices to the international architectural dialogue.

This year's Biennale theme – "Intelligens. Natural. Artificial. Collective." – explores how contemporary architecture addresses challenges from globalization and digitalization while preserving cultural characteristics. Macao, a city where Eastern and Western cultures intertwine, boasts heritage sites visible on nearly every corner. These structures, more than just buildings, stand as a testament to the cultural exchange between East and West. They witness the journey from initial encounters and understanding to mutual appreciation and integration within cultures. As a constantly evolving city, Macao continuously explores "intelligence" (wisdom), "nature" (the environment), "artificiality" (cultural creativity) and "collectivity" (social harmony), offering compelling interpretations of the Biennale's theme and bringing engaging contents and perspectives to the international creative dialogue.

In recent years, Macao has actively pursued its vision of becoming "one center, one platform, and one base," leveraging its advantages as a cultural crossroads between East and West to strengthen internal connections, foster external communications, and enhance multicultural exchange and integration. The 19th Venice International Architecture Biennale provides an invaluable platform for the city to

獻辭

柯嵐

澳門特別行政區政府
社會文化司司長

威尼斯國際建築雙年展，是世界著名的建築藝術和文化交流盛會。中國澳門自2014年首次參展以來，多次在雙年展上展示其獨特的文化魅力與建築智慧，為全球建築文化對話帶來新的聲音。

本屆建築雙年展以"智能、自然、人工、集體"為主題，聚焦當代建築如何在全球化與數字化中應對挑戰，保持文化特色。澳門是一座東西文化交融的城市，隨處可見的文物建築，不僅僅是磚石木瓦的堆砌，更是東西方文化交流共生的結晶，見證了不同文化從相遇、相識到相互欣賞、相互融合的美好歷程。同時，澳門也是一座一直在成長的城市，始終探索"智能"（智慧）、"自然"（環境）、"人工"（文化創造力）與"集體"（社會和諧），生動詮釋今年大會的主題，為這一國際對話增添深刻的內容與獨特的視角。

近年來，澳門積極推進"一中心、一平台、一基地"建設，發揮中西薈萃的獨特優勢，強化內聯外通作用，增進多元文化交流融合。第十九屆威尼斯國際建築雙年展為澳門提供了一個展示城市特色、加強國際交流合作的平台，使澳門更好地成為國家高水平對外開放的重要橋頭堡和中西文明交流互鑒的重要窗口。

本屆展會的澳門展區，由著名建築大師王澍教授及陸文宇教授擔任策展人，並由多位藝術家、建築師參與，通過照片及裝置形

showcase its urban character and promote international exchange and cooperation, further solidifying its role as a key gateway for China's high-level opening up and a vital window for exchange and mutual learning between Eastern and Western civilizations.

The Macao Exhibition at this year's Biennale is curated by renowned architects Professor Wang Shu and Professor Lu Wenyu, with contributions from numerous artists and architects. They use photographs and installations to transform Macao's multifaceted urban landscape into a poetic narrative of architectural language. I extend my sincere gratitude to the curatorial team and the participating artists and architects. Through their efforts, the "Exhibition from Macao, China" will open itself to the world like an intricately carved Lingnan window, revealing the charm of integrating Eastern and Western elements in Macao's architecture and urban development, profoundly inspiring a global audience.

I look forward to the Macao Exhibition shining brightly at this Biennale, showcasing the city's unique charm on the stage of architectural art, promoting intercultural dialogue and sharing engaging stories of China with the world.

I wish the exhibition great success.

式, 將澳門城市的多重面貌轉化為一場建築語言的詩意敘事。在此, 本人謹向策展團隊和參與的藝術家、建築師致以深深的感謝。相信在他們的努力下, 澳門展區將如一扇精心雕琢的嶺南窗扉, 向全球徐徐打開, 呈現出澳門建築與城市建設中西合璧的獨特魅力, 為全球觀眾帶來深刻的啟發。

期待澳門展區在此次雙年展中大放異彩, 在建築藝術的舞台上展現澳門風采, 推動文明對話, 向世界講好中國故事。

預祝展覽圓滿成功!

MESSAGE

Deland, Leong Wai Man

President of the Cultural Affairs Bureau of the
Macao Special Administrative Region Government

With the theme "Intelligens. Natural. Artificial. Collective." this year's Venice International Architecture Biennale is a profound reflection on architecture's role in globalization. The urban fabric of Macao presents a complex "cultural landscape," where historical buildings and modern urban spaces create a parallel narrative of time and space. Here, tradition and modernity coexist while also engaging in dialogue and interaction, forming a unique urban realm that responds to the theme of this Biennale.

For this year's edition, we have the distinct honor of having internationally renowned architects Wang Shu and Lu Wenyu as our curators. Their unique perspective will transform the multiple facets of Macao's cityscape into a poetic architectural narrative. They divide Macao into four "parallel worlds": the depth of the historical town; the symbolic meanings of casino architecture that blends East and West; the geometric order of the modern city; and the future projection of a digital, intangible city. These four parallel worlds resemble four mirror images, reflecting the ways in which Macao maintains the foundations of its culture in the waves of globalization while embracing the future with an open attitude.

Among the exhibited works, renowned architectural photographer Iwan Baan captures pieces of memories and the contemporary vitality of Macao's urban spaces through his highly narrative imagery. Furthermore, architecture students and professors from the China Academy of Art and the University of Saint Joseph in Macao have transformed their

獻辭

梁惠敏

澳門特別行政區政府
文化局局長

本屆威尼斯國際建築雙年展以"智能、自然、人工、集體"為主題，是一場對建築在全球化進程中角色的深刻反思。澳門的城市肌理，猶如一個錯綜複雜的"文化地景"，歷史建築與現代城市空間共同構築出一種平行的時空敘事。在這裡，傳統與現代不僅同時存在，更在對話、互動，形成一個獨特的城市場域，回應著本屆雙年展的主題。

為此，我們特邀國際著名建築師王澍與陸文宇擔任策展人，將澳門城市的多重面貌轉化為一場建築語言的詩意敘事。澳門被劃分為四個"平行世界"：歷史老城的縱深空間、中西合璧的賭場建築的符號象徵、現代新城的幾何秩序，以及數字化無形城市的未來投影。四個平行世界像四重鏡像，折射出澳門如何在全球化浪潮中保持自身文化的根基，同時以開放的姿態擁抱未來。在具體展品中，著名建築攝影師伊萬·巴恩以其極具敘事性的影像語言，捕捉澳門城市空間的斑駁記憶與當代活力。中國美術學院與澳門聖若瑟大學兩所院校的建築專業師生，則以裝置形式將學術思想轉化為與觀眾對話的空間體驗。

澳門是不同文明和諧相處、融合發展的典範，具有中西薈萃的文化優勢，是促進國際人文交流，講好中國故事，打造中西文明交流互鑒的重要窗口。參與威尼斯建築雙年展，正是澳門踐行這

academic ideas into spatial experiences that actively engage in dialogue with the audience through installations.

Macao is a model of harmonious coexistence and the integrated development of different civilizations, boasting a unique cultural advantage that blends both Eastern and Western influences – making the city a platform for promoting international cultural exchanges, narrating compelling Chinese stories, and facilitating mutual learning between Chinese and Western civilizations. Participation in the Venice International Architecture Biennale demonstrates Macao's commitment to this cultural mission on an international stage.

This exhibition from Macao weaves cultural memories and imagination of the future into a dynamic spatial narrative, allowing audiences to re-examine the relationship between architecture and culture at the interstices of history and modernity. We believe that under the curation of Wang Shu and Lu Wenyu, and with the collaborative efforts of Iwan Baan and architectural teams from both regions, this exhibition will deliver another brilliant interpretation of multicultural integration for the Biennale, further highlighting Macao's role as a bridge between cultures and enhancing the brand of the international city of "Macao, China."

I would like to extend my best wishes for the successful participation of Macao, China at the Venice International Architecture Biennale 2025. I look forward to seeing Macao radiate even more brightly internationally, showcasing its diverse architectural wisdom and cultural narratives.

一文化使命的國際化實踐。澳門展區將文化記憶與未來想像編織為一個動態的空間敘事，讓觀眾在歷史與現代的縫隙中，重新審視建築與文化的關係。我們相信，在王澍與陸文宇的策劃下，在伊萬·巴恩以及兩地建築學術團隊的共同努力下，澳門展區將可為本屆雙年展帶來多元文化交融的又一次精彩詮釋，進一步彰顯澳門內聯外通的角色功能，讓“中國澳門”國際大都市的品牌更加亮麗。

本人謹預祝中國澳門展區在2025年威尼斯國際建築雙年展上取得圓滿成功，並期待澳門以多元的建築智慧與文化敘事，在國際舞台上綻放更加耀眼的光芒。

PARALLEL WORLDS

Wang Shu & Lu Wenyu

Macao is a city on the south coast of China that is exceptional. It is known to the outside world as the "Las Vegas of the East," but for its residents it is an old, sixteenth-century trading port. Fortunately, the old city has been almost completely preserved. What is often overlooked by tourists, and other visitors from China and around the world, is that this seemingly small city also has a huge new "twin."

After Macao's return to China in 1999, it underwent a round of leapfrogging development. It can be said that because of its special history and location, Macao is not only an East Asian tourist hotspot, a node for cultural exchanges between the East and the West and a platform for cross-cultural cooperation in the region but, beyond all this, it is facing confusion and encountering challenges. In the face of successive huge waves of globalization and the evolution of digitalization and intelligence, is it still possible for Macao to maintain its own cultural characteristics? How can globalized development and digital intelligence solve its various social contradictions and problems? Besides being swept along by urban development, is there any room for creative development in Macao?

In our opinion, the most confusing and interesting thing about Macao is that this not-so-big city seems to be composed of several cities side by side. These multiple cities are so different in character that they seem to have nothing to do with each other; nonetheless – and incredibly – they coexist peacefully. A visitor who had been here before Macao's return to China in 1999, who had frequented the old Casino Lisboa,

平行世界

王澍 & 陸文宇

澳門是中國南部沿海的一個足夠特殊的城市。對於整個世界來說，它最著名的稱呼是"東方的拉斯維加斯"，但對於澳門本地居民，這是一個自16世紀以來的老城，幸運的是，這個老城幾乎被完整的保存下來。對於從中國和世界各地來澳門的旅遊者和訪問者來說，經常忽略的是，這個看似不大的城市還有一個巨大的新城，在澳門1999年回歸中國後，這個城市經歷了一輪大躍進式的發展。可以說，澳門因為它特殊的歷史和位置，不僅是亞洲東部的一個旅遊熱點城市，是東西方文化交流的一個節點，是所在區域的一個跨文化合作的平臺，但除此之外，這個城市也面臨困惑，在巨大的全球化發展中，在整個世界的數位化、智慧化的演進浪潮中，澳門還有沒有保持自身文化特色的可能?這種發展和智慧化如何能夠解決各種社會矛盾和問題？除了被發展所裹挾，澳門有沒有創造性發展的空間？

在我們看來，澳門最讓訪問者困惑，也是它最有意思的地方，是這個不大的城市，似乎是有多個城市並列構成的。這若干城中之城，彼此差異如此之大，似乎毫不相干，但又不可思議的和平共處。一個在1999年澳門回歸中國之前訪問過這裡的訪客，一個曾經訪問過老葡京賭場的訪客，一定會為新葡京大廈和澳門老城的巨大的尺度反差所震撼。而一個熟悉澳門歷史的訪客，也一

would surely be shocked by the huge contrast between the new tower of the Grand Lisboa and the old city of Macao. And a visitor who was familiar with the history of Macao would also be shocked by the scale and size of the new city on the island of Hengqin, because it seems to come from some completely different world in parallel time and space.

If we call the old city of Macao, this area where time seems to flow slowly, "World 1: Old Town" (it can, in fact, almost be called a kind of "nature"), then the series of newly built, huge casino buildings represented by MGM and the Grand Lisboa tower, a kind of "collective" of a backdrop-style city representing the powerful forces of capital, can be called "World 2: Casino City." The new city on Hengqin Island represents the whole world's obsession with and overconfidence in "modern" cities and buildings since the turn of the twentieth century – and it displays a super-cultural, super-human construction model, scale and lifestyle. This we can call "World 3: New City," but what is easily overlooked is that the digital operation in the new city is invisible: like all cities in China, Macao is also a cashless city – and we can call this invisible city "World 4: Digital City."

This coexistence of four worlds is what makes Macao so extraordinary. It could be argued that across Asia, reality is often more shocking than fiction. Macao's cultural influence is immense; it can be said that not only is it named the "Las Vegas of the East" but also that hundreds of cities throughout China and Southeast Asia are the result (to co-opt Robert Venturi and Denise Scott Brown's famous phrase) of "learning from Las Vegas." The harmonious coexistence of several completely different cities serves as the secret code to the region's history and culture, while the uncertain collision between parallel worlds implied by these cities may stimulate all kinds of creative forces.

定會被橫琴粵澳深度合作區的新城的規模和尺度所震撼。因為這幾個城市似乎來自平行時空中完全不同的世界。如果我們把澳門老城，這個時間緩慢流過的區域稱之為"世界1"，它幾乎可以被稱為一種"自然"，那麼，以美高梅、新葡京為代表的一系列新建的巨大賭場建築，一種代表資本強大力量的佈景式城市的"集體"，就可以稱之為"世界2"，而橫琴島上的新城所代表的，則是整個世界20世紀以來對"現代性"城市與建築的迷思與過度自信，發展出一種超文化，超人類的建設模式、尺度、生活方式，這種"集體"我們稱之為"世界3"，但是，容易被忽略的是，城市的數位化運行是看不見的，比如和中國所有城市一樣，澳門也是一個無現金城市，我們可以把這個看不見的城市稱之為"世界4"。

正是這四種城市不可思議並存的現實讓人震撼。可以說，在整個亞洲，現實經常比虛構更加讓人震撼。澳門的特殊之處在於它巨大的文化影響，可以說，不僅澳門是"東方的拉斯維加斯"，整個中國和東南亞有上百個城市是"向拉斯維加斯學習"的結果。若干完全不同的城市和平共處是這個地區歷史與文化的密碼，而這些城市所意味著的平行世界之間的不確定的衝擊則可能誘發各種創造性的力量。

BETWEEN WORLDS

Wang Shu

As co-curators of the Macao Exhibition at the Venice International Architecture Biennale this year, Lu Wenyu and I share a profound impression of Macao from recent years: a relatively small city that – due to its unique historical background, geographical environment and developmental trajectory – has brought diverse and contrasting worlds closely together. In other words, urban realities that seem incompatible in everyday life have coincidentally collided here.

Given this complexity, we determined that perceptive photography would best capture this distinctive sensation. Nevertheless, architects with the required "sense of worlds" have always been few, and architectural photographers who can capture these simultaneous realities are equally rare. Henri Cartier-Bresson's photographs come to mind, as they often portray this consciousness – portraits frequently composed vertically, positioning people near the bottom with other clearly depicted objects above, creating an impression of two coexisting worlds.

Among contemporary architectural photographers familiar to us, the first to come to mind who embodies such consciousness is Iwan Baan. In 2007, commissioned by *Domus* magazine, Iwan Baan photographed the second phase of our Xiangshan Campus project at the China Academy of Art in Hangzhou. His images left a deep impression on us; they were markedly different from typical architectural photography, which often emphasizes aesthetics, absence of people and monumental composition. His photographs consistently include people, capturing scenes as if an event has just

在世界之間

王澍

我和陸文宇作為今年威尼斯國際建築雙年展中國澳門展區的聯合策展人，我們對澳門這個城市近幾年的一致的最深印象是，一個不大的城市，卻因為它特殊的歷史位置、地理環境和演變邏輯，將幾個區別很大的生活世界高密度的並置在一起。或者說，生活中不可能在一起的城市事物似乎偶然的就碰撞在一起了。

作為策展人，我們覺得應該用一種敏銳的攝影去捕捉這種感覺。但是，有這種“世界感”的建築師從來都不多，能夠抓拍到這種多世界平行狀態的建築攝影師也同樣很少。印象裡布列松的攝影中有這種意識，他的人像攝影中經常看到這樣一種構圖，人在豎構圖的下部分，一些事物在上部分，它們同樣清晰，似乎是同時存在的兩個世界。而在我們熟悉的建築攝影師中，尋找有這種意識的，我們首先想到的就是伊萬·巴恩。他在2007年為我們業餘建築工作室剛剛完成的杭州中國美術學院象山校園二期拍攝了一組照片，記得當時是《Domus》雜誌的約稿，這組照片讓我們印象深刻。和常見的那種唯美的、沒有人的、紀念性構圖的建築攝影不同，他的照片中總是有人存在的，似乎是在現實中某種事件剛剛發生時被抓住的一個場景。但是作為一個專業的建築攝影師，不管事件如何發生，建築和城市本身的平行存在仍然是清晰有力的。對這種特殊時刻的特殊場景的發現，他的意識非常敏銳，

occurred in real life. He thus captures the parallel existence of architecture and urban context in a way that remains clear and powerful regardless of the unfolding events. His acute awareness in identifying special scenes at special moments is reminiscent of Henri Cartier-Bresson's approach. Another essential aspect of Iwan Baan's work is his understanding of the parallel relationship between architecture and its (often natural) environment. Most architectural and urban photography places architecture at the center, but Iwan highlights the equal significance of architecture, environment and nature – a perspective closely aligned with our design philosophy. He perceives cities through the simultaneous presence of permanence and change, and he grasps both the overall and detailed aspects involved. From single buildings to extensive urban environments, his images collectively offer a rich and compelling portrayal.

The public might not realize that architects and urban planners often begin their designs from an aerial perspective, using bird's-eye sketches and models. As an architectural photographer, Iwan pays particular attention to capturing views from above. This approach is not only spatial but also temporal, reflecting Iwan's keen interest in documenting the city's daily transitions, from dawn through dusk to nighttime.

Experiencing architecture or a city from both ground level and aerial perspectives fully reveals its distinctive qualities and charm. Iwan Baan's photographs for the Macao Exhibition offered a selection of outstanding images. Reviewing these images, I find Macao to be a fascinating place whose changes mirror the complexities of our world, suggesting an uncertain yet meaningful future.

很有點布列松的風範。另外一個重要的視角是他能夠理解建築與環境的平行關係。大多數建築與城市攝影都是默認以建築為中心的, 而伊萬·巴恩能夠理解我們的作品中那種建築與環境與自然的平等意識, 多樣性事物的並行存在的意識。或者說, 他對於城市的認識, 他有著一種對不變與變化的事物同時存在的認識, 對整體與細節同時把握的認識。所以他拍攝一個對象, 無論是一個建築還是一個城市, 他的照片能夠形成一組獨特且豐富的呈現。

一般公眾也許不知道, 建築師、城市規劃師在設計的初始, 往往是從天上的視角開始。總平面圖, 總體模型都是從一種俯瞰的草圖開始。作為一個建築攝影師, 伊萬特別注重用航空攝影捕捉俯瞰場景。這不僅是一種空間視角, 也是一種時間視角, 伊萬特別注重追尋一個城市從清晨到日落到夜晚的變化。

將地上的視角和天上的視角同時去看, 一個建築、一座城市的特質與魅力才會完整展現。

這次伊萬·巴恩為澳門館拍攝的澳門城市的一組作品, 有足夠多的好照片讓我們選擇, 讓人興奮。看了這些照片, 我最基本的感覺是, 澳門是如此有意思的地方, 它的變化折射著這個複雜世界的變化, 這種變化預示著一個不確定但是有意義的未來。

LISBOA

OLD TOWN

老城

Old Town 老城
Casino City 賭城
New City 新城

The most captivating part of Macao is its main island, at the heart of which lies the old town. Before Macao's return from Portuguese administration to China in 1999, new urban areas had already been developed on its outer island – and, following the return, extensive development began on Hengqin Island, which is connected to the Chinese mainland. However, the modernist urban plans and architecture of these developments are similar to those seen elsewhere in Asia and around the world, making them present in Macao but not uniquely *of* Macao. Only on the main island can one trace Macao's full development from a Chinese fishing village into today's modern city.

Remarkably, Macao's old town is exceptionally well preserved. Given the small size of the main island, the old town covers most of its area, pushing the globally famous casino buildings to the island's edges or onto reclaimed land. If you take your time exploring it on foot or by bicycle, you will discover numerous surprises – although it may be challenging at times due to the steep terrain, as the buildings follow the contours of the hills. Most of the buildings in the old town are four- or five-story European-style structures, some reaching seven or eight stories, originating from the Portuguese influence that began in the sixteenth century. The old town actually consists of two parts: a Chinese town and a Portuguese town. Although traditional Chinese single-story courtyard buildings have largely disappeared, except for temples, remnants of the original dividing walls between the two towns remain, creating unique residences built into the walls themselves. These walls essentially follow a north–south ridge, with the Chinese town facing the mainland and the Portuguese residential area facing the ocean. Most striking, however, is the coexistence of several different worlds. Through gaps in the somewhat dilapidated buildings in "World 1: Old Town," one suddenly glimpses the dazzling casino buildings in "World 2: Casino City," twenty times the scale, gleaming as if from another historical dimension; or new high-rise buildings from "World 3: New City," symbolizing a decisive break with history. Yet everything appears calm and orderly, daily life unfolding quietly without apparent contradiction.

澳門最有魅力的地方就是它的本島。本島的核心就是澳門老城。當然, 澳門在1999年回歸中國前已經在它的外島建設了新城, 回歸後, 又在和大陸銜接的橫琴島進行了大規模的開發建設, 但是, 這種現代主義風格的新城規劃和建築在整個亞洲整個世界的各地都類似可見, 可以說它們在澳門但是並不是澳門。只有在本島, 我們可以看到澳門從一個中國漁村到今天現代都市的完整發展脈絡。讓人驚喜的是, 澳門的老城保護得非常完整。本島不大, 老城覆蓋了它的大部分, 這使得澳門聞名世界的賭城建築只能沿本島邊緣建造, 或者只能使用填海造地。局部的新城規劃與新建築, 估計是因為投資成本, 主要是高層建築, 也是被擠壓在邊緣。可以想像, 這三種力量是如何博弈的。同時, 保護老城的力量又是如何的強大。如果你仔細地, 慢慢地閱讀老城, 步行或者騎自行車, 你會發現更多驚喜。也會有點辛苦, 因為老城是圍繞著一個山丘而建, 建築都是順應地形建造, 有些地方高差相當大。老城的建築大部分是四、五層, 七、八層的歐洲風格的建築, 是16世紀開始因葡萄牙人的到來而興起。它實際上包括中國城和葡萄牙城兩部分。儘管中國式的單層院落房屋, 除了廟宇之外, 基本看不到了, 但是當初分隔兩部分的城牆在很多地方仍然保存著, 並且形成了利用城牆修建的特殊住宅。這個城牆基本沿南北走向的山脊建造, 中國城面向大陸, 葡萄牙居住區面向大洋。但是最讓人訝異的景觀仍然是幾個世界的並存。從老城這個世界1的有些殘舊的建築縫隙中, 你會突然看見代表世界2的賭城建築, 它是20倍尺度的存在, 閃閃發光, 似乎是來自另一個世界的歷史。或者是代表世界3的高層新建築, 代表著和歷史切斷關係的決絕態度。但是一切都如此乾淨和平靜, 生活慢慢的發生著, 似乎沒有任何矛盾。

ESCOLA PORTUGUESA
DE
MACAU
澳門葡文學校

後門出入
禁止放置雜物

業投資有限公司
傳真:2878 0369

禁止吸煙
MOP$1500

AIA

9

RUA DO INTERIOR

1

十月初五馬路
AVENIDA DE
CINCO DE OUTUBRO

3

36-A

致各位街坊朋友
多谢合作

BECO DA OSTRA

bauhaus
Columbia
代理出租
6646-6615
6610-7590
高溫清洗冷氣
家電維修

1

興
各位君子

warning
禁止倚靠
注意安全
POST

1

POOH
MM 45-06
ML 34-65
MM 63-84

CHAN
SU
TAK
MU
54-18
MO
75-26

SUN TAI ON 3
新泰安叁
BM21535Y
PERDUE Chicken Franks

25
45

S.T.D.M.NO.8

MN-97-11

一綫天

5

SAÍDA

春秋垂訓

德流光莆田福曜

6876-3095
6627-2127

大鐵棚
食堂
OPEN

啟思
補習/教育中心

.03

DOCA D. CARLOS I

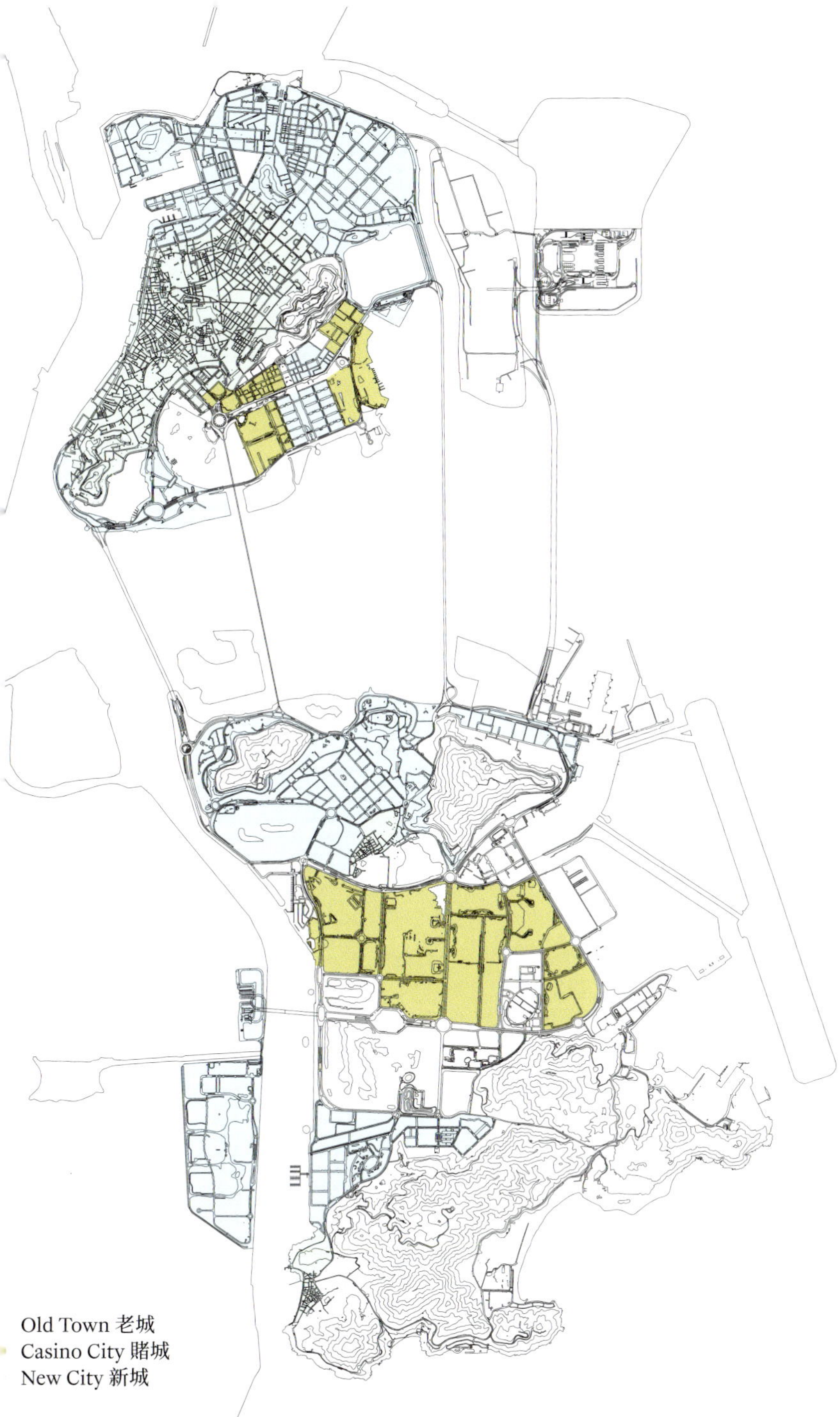

Old Town 老城
Casino City 賭城
New City 新城

If the human scale and everyday life of Macao's old town move you, then you will undoubtedly be stunned by the casino architecture on the city's main island. Stepping out from the edge of the old town, crossing just a single street, you may suddenly face a high-rise building twenty or even a hundred times the scale of those you have left behind. Its scale bears no relation to the old town, as it is constructed to satisfy desires inflated dozens or hundreds of times beyond ordinary life. If you had visited Macao's casino city before its return to China in 1999, you would have found that while casino buildings were the largest, tallest and most luxurious structures on the periphery, they still maintained some connection in scale and cultural aesthetics with the old town.

However, the casino buildings constructed after the return have completely severed ties with local history. You soon realize their points of reference and competition lie not in Macao but far away in Las Vegas, as if these new casinos had been parachuted into place. Interestingly, unlike modernist architecture, casino buildings often incorporate historical elements – luxurious, exaggerated and possessing a special sense of scale – as though simplified historical architecture or artifacts have been magnified a hundredfold, resulting in an explosive visual impact. When ordinary people accidentally interact with these casinos, their posture and daily lives juxtaposed against the grandeur of the architecture create an uncanny sense of displacement. If you ask an average Macao resident about their feelings toward the casinos, they might respond, "We usually just pretend they don't exist."

如果說你在澳門老城會為那種人的尺度和普通人的日常生活而感動, 那麼你一定會被澳門本島上的賭城建築而震驚。從老城邊緣走出來, 只過一條馬路, 你就可能直面一個二十倍甚至一百倍尺度的高層建築。它完全在尺度上和老城沒有關係, 或者說, 它是為比普通生活膨脹幾十倍或者上百倍的欲望而建造的。如果你在1999年澳門回歸中國之前到訪過這裡的賭城, 你會發現, 賭城建築肯定是老城邊緣最大最高最豪華的, 但是它們的尺度和文化趣味和老城仍然有關, 但是回歸後新建造的賭城建築, 和這裡的歷史完全脫節了。於是你意識到, 它們的參照物件和競爭物件已經不在這裡, 而在遙遠的拉斯維加斯。這些新的賭城是空降到這裡的。有意思的是, 和那些現代主義的新建築不同, 賭城建築喜歡帶一些歷史元素, 那種豪華的、誇張的, 並且有一種特殊的尺度感, 似乎是把一個被簡化的歷史建築或者工藝品直接放大了一百倍, 有一種特別直接的爆發力。有意思的是, 當普通人偶然誤入賭城, 他們的身體姿態和生活狀態和宏大的建築並置, 就有種莫名的錯位感。如果你問一個普通澳門人, 他或者她對賭城的態度, 他們可能會說:我們平常就當它們不存在。

HEIGHT LIMIT 3.6m

ASCOTT

DFA

德勝押
便利店
祥勝押
國內卡
祥勝押

CASINO
LISBOA

益豐美食

MZ-32-84

POLICIA

勵庭海景

吃不停 · 购不尽 免费泊车
吃不停 · 购不尽 免费泊车
Shop and Dine with free parking

22

MGM 美高梅

ENETI

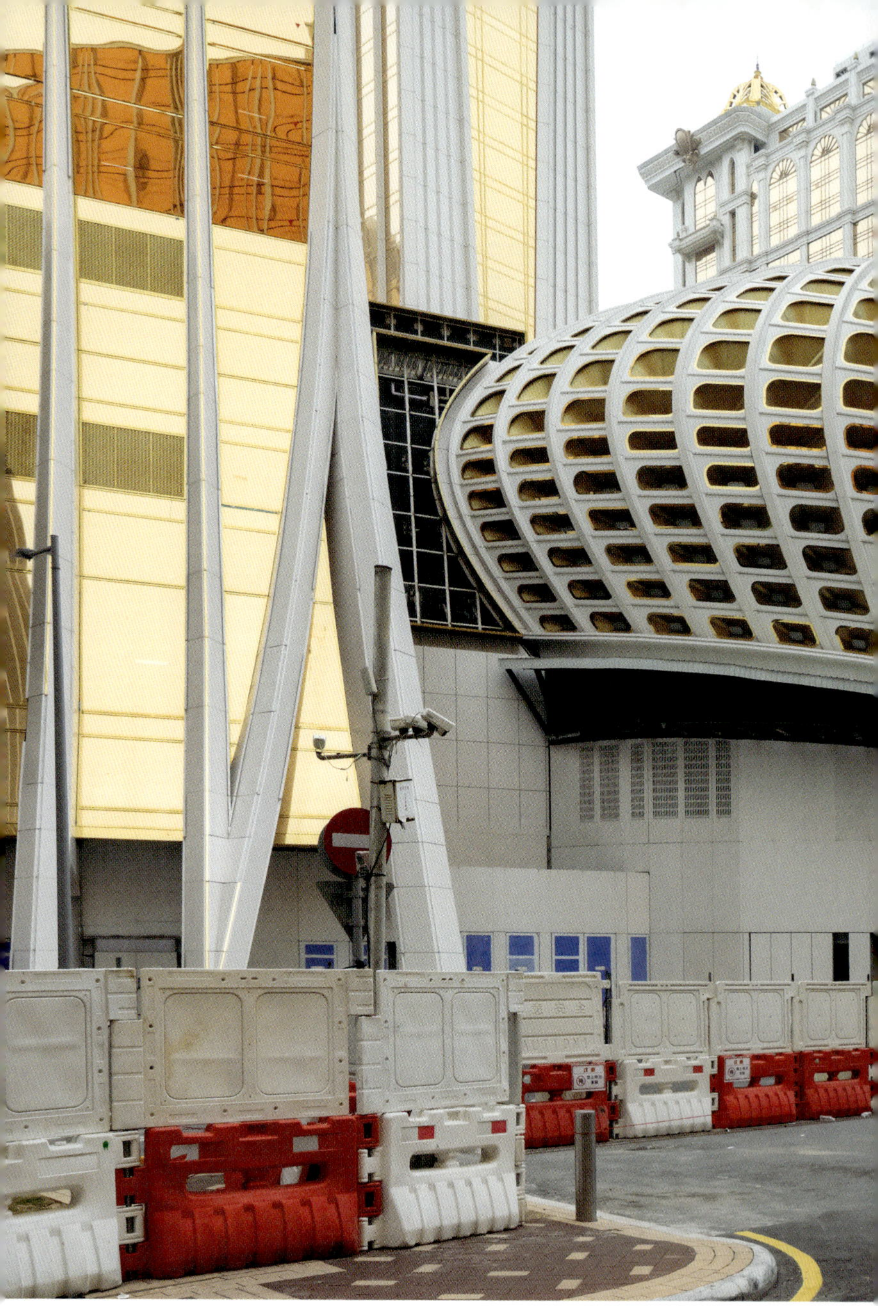

40
Z-135

消防喉轆
FIRE HOSE REEL

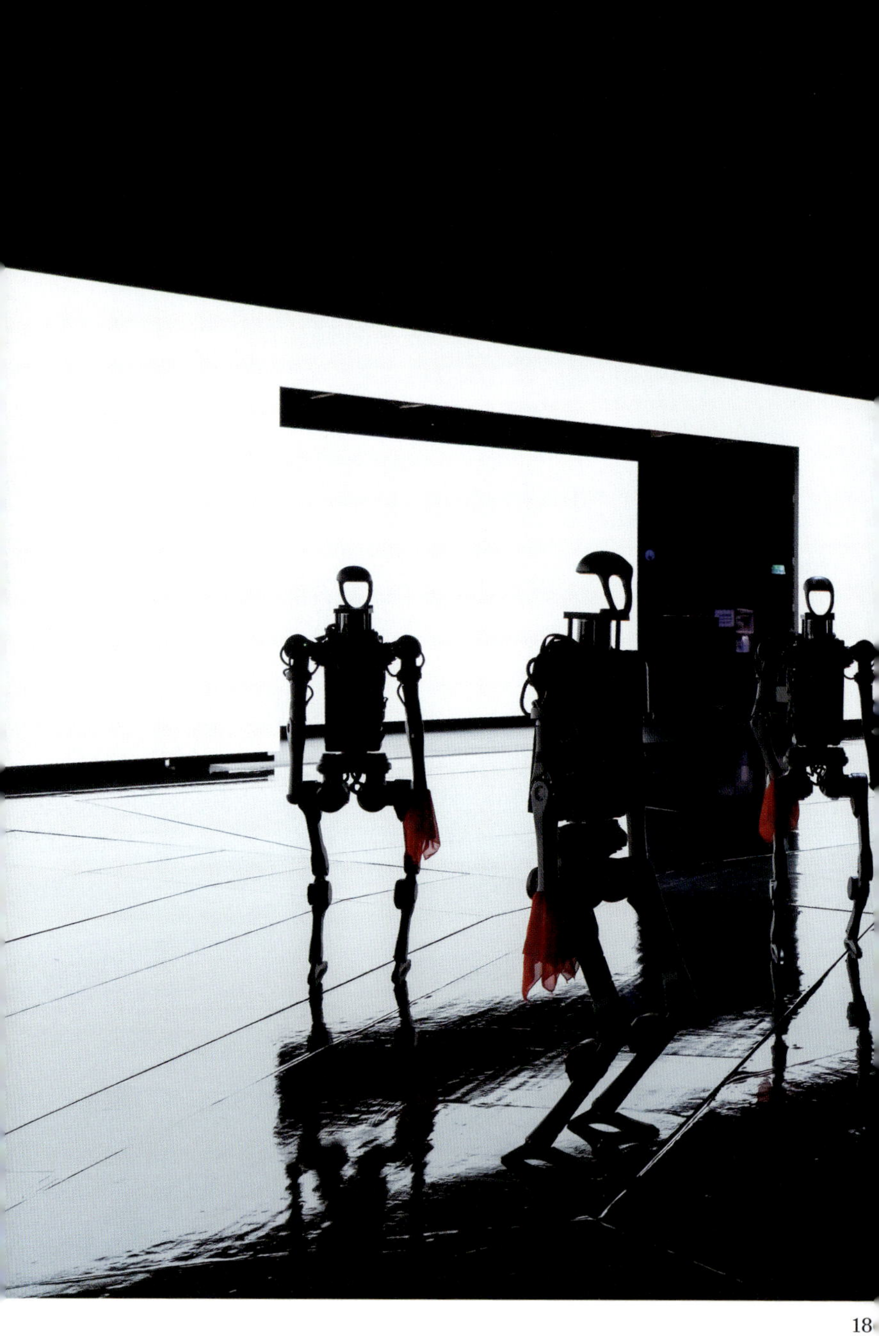

AIAAIA

GRAND LISBOA

NEW CITY

新城

Old Town 老城
Casino City 賭城
New City 新城

On Macao's main island, one can witness both the continuous evolution and sudden transformations in architecture from the sixteenth century to the present. For architectural historians, Macao serves as an exceptionally valuable research case. In many other East Asian cities, historical continuity is often fragmented or incomplete; in Macao, however, this evolution remains largely intact. You will find that the old town has continually evolved, from one- or two-story buildings to structures seven or eight stories tall, shifting significantly in both building typology and style. In contrast, the modern, new city, in terms of planning and architecture, represents a radical departure – a sudden and unnatural break from history and everyday life, spreading rapidly and artificially. These new urban developments, typically large in scale, appear neutral and generic, lacking distinctive local characteristics. Regardless of their design, the traces of rapid, short-term planning and construction are evident.

They share a common feature: an unwelcoming environment for pedestrians, characterized as they are by fragmented and disconnected pathways. Although planners claim rational and meticulous consideration has gone into these developments, such overly confident planning often neglects human-scale detail. Ultimately, urban charm can only emerge from historical and cultural accumulation – it cannot be manufactured instantly. Frequently, what alleviates the monotony of modern buildings are the spontaneous actions of daily life, such as the metal cages installed on balconies for safety in modern Asian residential buildings. Since residents install these individually, the resulting urban landscape is similar yet subtly varied.

在澳門本島, 你可以看到從16世紀到今天, 建築的連續演變史和突變史。如果你是一個建築史學者, 澳門是一個特別好的研究樣本。在其他東亞城市, 這種演變的歷史部分基本都是破碎狀態, 殘缺不全, 但是澳門是完整的。你會發現, 老城是一直在演變的, 從一兩層到七八層, 從建築的類型到風格。但是現代的新城, 無論是規劃還是建築, 完全是一種突變, 一種完全脫離歷史, 脫離正常生活的變化過程的突變, 一種完全不自然的現象發生並快速蔓延。這些新城尺度同樣巨大, 通常以一種中性的樣式呈現, 沒有屬性, 不管如何設計, 都無法擺脫短期快速設計快速建造的痕跡。它們還有一個共同特徵, 對在那裡以步行的方式遊蕩是不友好的, 路徑是不連貫的, 儘管聲稱經過了理性的周密考慮, 但是這種過度自信的規劃似乎通常照顧不到人這麼細膩的尺度。你會發現, 城市的魅力只能來自於歷史的沉澱和文化的積累, 魅力是無法短期製造的。能夠改變這種現代建築的無趣現象的經常是人們日常生活行為, 比如為了安全, 這種亞洲現代住宅建築陽臺上加裝的金屬籠, 因為是每戶自己加的, 所以相似又不同。

封
頂
大
20
15
10
5

出境大堂
P

MS
70-99
ZN 9307

封頂
大吉

09

377

28785939
籠包 餡餅 牛肉麵
24小時營業
台灣美食
FAMOUS
MACAU
您專業的
時尚顧問

2.20 m

MX
24-44
MR
48-14

BANCO TAI FUNG
24

"World 4," the digital city, is omnipresent yet invisible – and it may decisively shape our future.

世界4, 數字之城, 它已經無處不在, 它是看不見的, 但是它可能決定性地影響著我們的未來。

系統故障-請重新啟動
停止
系統故障-請重新啟動
停止
系統錯誤
系統故障-請重新啟動
停止
SYSTEM ERROR
ERROR_NOT_ENOUGH_MEMORY
OK
系統錯誤
系統故障-請重新啟動
停止
系統錯誤
系統故障-請重新啟動
停止

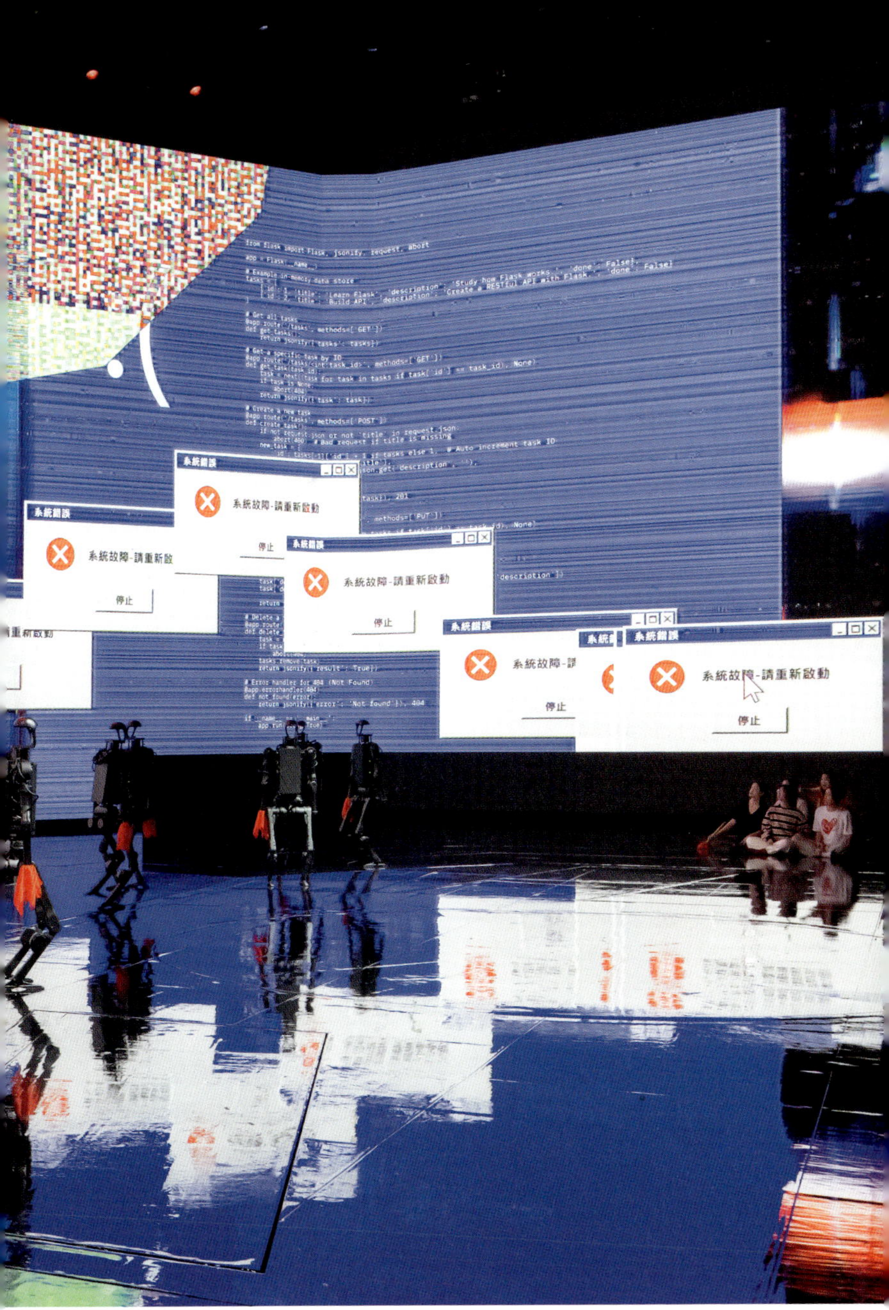
系統錯誤
系統故障-請重新啟動
停止

CONTRIBUTORS

Wang Shu and *Lu Wenyu* are architects and educators. In 1997, they co-founded Amateur Architecture Studio in Hangzhou, China. Together, the two also founded the architecture department at the China Academy of Art in 2003. In response to the reality of rapid urban development and the massive demolition of traditional buildings in China, they create new explorations in contemporary Chinese architecture. In their work, they have committed themselves to the research and practice of reconstructing contemporary Chinese architecture, which is reflected in their built projects such as the National Archives of Publications and Culture in Hangzhou, the Ningbo Historic Museum and the Xiangshan Campus of the China Academy of Art, which in 2021 was named one of "The 25 Most Significant Works of Postwar Architecture" worldwide by *The New York Times*. Instead of simply imitating traditional styles, their goal is to reconnect tradition with the contemporary.

Wang Shu is Dean of the Architecture School at the China Academy of Art. In projects such as the Ningbo Historic Museum, he has experimented with a new way of building by recycling demolished traditional building materials mixed with modern materials and techniques. In 2006, he designed the TILES GARDEN for the first China Pavilion at the Venice International Architecture Biennale and has subsequently been awarded numerous prizes. He was the 2012 Pritzker Architecture Prize Laureate and, in 2023, was elected as a member of the French Academy of Architecture.

Lu Wenyu received the Schelling Architecture Prize in Germany and an Honorary Award from the Venice Biennale in 2010. She was the recipient of the 2019 Gold Medal of Tau Sigma Delta and, in 2023, was elected as a member of the French Academy of Architecture. From 2020 to 2023, she was the juror of the UNESCO Asia-Pacific Awards for Cultural Heritage Conservation.

Iwan Baan is a Dutch photographer based in Amsterdam and the US, known primarily for images that narrate the life and interactions occurring within architecture. With no formal architectural training, Baan takes photographs that reflect the questions and perspectives of the everyday individuals who give meaning and context to the architecture and spaces that surround us. His artistic approach has given matters of architecture an approachable and accessible voice. In 2012, he received the Golden Lion at the Venice Biennale for his work on the Torre David in Caracas, Venezuela, gaining him further international acclaim. Architects turn to Baan to give their work a sense of place and narrative within its environments.

策展人及藝術家

建築師、教育家**王澍**和**陸文宇**於1997年在中國杭州一起創建業餘建築工作室。2003 年他們在中國美術學院共同創辦建築系。他們針對城市高速發展與傳統建築被大量拆毀的現實，試圖開創一種當代中國建築的新探索。他們一起致力於重新構築中國當代建築的研究和實踐，在不模仿傳統樣式的基礎上，將傳統與今天重新聯繫起來。這體現在他們所創作的眾多作品中，如:杭州國家版本館、寧波博物館和中國美術學院象山校園，這座校園在2021年入選了《紐約時報》全球“二戰以來最重要的25個建築”之一。

王澍，中國美術學院建築學院院長，在寧波博物館這樣的作品中，他嘗試了一種通過回收被拆毀的傳統建築材料與現代材料及工藝混合建造的新方式。2006年，他設計了威尼斯雙年展國際建築展首屆中國國家館“瓦園”，此後，他獲得一系列國際建築獎。2012年，他獲得普利茲克建築獎。2023年，他被授予法國建築科學院外籍院士。

陸文宇曾榮獲德國謝林建築實踐大獎、2010年威尼斯雙年展特別榮譽獎、2019年北美TSD 建築教育聯盟金質獎章。2023年，她被授予法蘭西建築科學院院士。從2020年到2023年，她是聯合國教科文組織亞太地區文化遺產保護獎評委。

伊萬 · 巴恩(Iwan Baan)是一位荷蘭攝影師，常駐於阿姆斯特丹和美國，以擅長拍攝建築內部生活與互動的影像而聞名。巴恩雖未受過正規的建築訓練，卻能透過攝影捕捉日常生活中普通人的疑問與視角，這些人為我們周遭的建築與空間賦予了意義和脈絡。他的藝術手法為建築議題帶來了平易近人且易於理解的聲音。2012年，他因拍攝委內瑞拉加拉加斯的大衛塔(Torre David)而在威尼斯雙年展上榮獲金獅獎，這進一步提升了他的國際聲譽。建築師們尋求與巴恩合作，以賦予他們的作品一種場所感以及與環境相融的敘事。